FIGHT

STUDY GUIDE

Also by Craig Groeschel

Altar Ego: Becoming Who God Says You Are

*Chazown: Define Your Vision. Pursue Your Passion.
Live Your Life on Purpose.*

*The Christian Atheist: Believing in God
but Living as If He Doesn't Exist*

Dare to Drop the Pose
(previously titled *Confessions of a Pastor*)

Love, Sex, and Happily Ever After
(previously titled *Going All the Way*)

It: How Churches and Leaders Can Get It and Keep It

Soul Detox: Clean Living in a Contaminated World

Weird: Because Normal Isn't Working

What Is God Really Like? (general editor)

FIGHT

WINNING THE BATTLES THAT MATTER MOST

CRAIG GROESCHEL

with Judson Poling

ZONDERVAN®

ZONDERVAN

Fight Study Guide
Copyright © 2013 by Craig Groeschel

This title is also available as a Zondervan ebook. Visit www.zondervan.com/ebooks.

Requests for information should be addressed to:

Zondervan, *Grand Rapids, Michigan 49530*

ISBN 978-0-310-89496-4

Craig Groeschel is represented by Thomas J. Winters and Jeffrey C. Dunn of Winters, King, & Associates, Inc., Tulsa, Oklahoma.

Cover design: Dual Identity
Cover photo: Alfonse Pagano / Getty Images®
Interior images: Dual Identity
Interior design: Sarah Johnson with Beth Shagene

Printed in the United States of America

16 17 18 19 /RRD/ 21 20 19 18 17 16 15 14 13 12 11 10 9 8 7

CONTENTS

HOW TO USE THIS GUIDE

Group Size

The *Fight* video curriculum is designed to be experienced in a group setting such as a men's Bible study or men's Sunday school class. To ensure everyone has enough time to participate in discussions, large groups may want to break up into smaller groups of four to six people each.

Materials Needed

Each participant should have his study guide, which includes notes for video segments, directions for activities and discussion questions, as well as personal studies to deepen learning between sessions.

Timing

There is enough material for each session to last an hour—approximately 20 minutes for the video and 40 minutes for opening remarks, discussion, and closing prayer. If you have a longer meeting, you may wish to allow more time for discussion and activities.

Facilitation

Each group should appoint a facilitator who is responsible for starting the video and for keeping track of time during discussions and activities. Facilitators may also read questions aloud and monitor discussions, prompting participants to respond and assuring that everyone has the opportunity to participate.

Personal Study

Maximize the impact of the curriculum with additional study between group sessions. Every personal study includes reflection questions, Bible study, and a guided prayer activity. You'll get the most out of the curriculum by setting aside about one hour between sessions for personal study. For each session, you may wish to complete the personal study all in one sitting or to spread it out over a few days.

OF NOTE

The quotations interspersed throughout this study guide are excerpts from the book *Fight* by Craig Groeschel. All other resources — including discussion questions and personal studies — have been written by Judson Poling in collaboration with Craig Groeschel.

FIGHT LIKE A MAN

I see in Fight Club the strongest and smartest men who've ever lived. I see all this potential, and I see squandering. An entire generation pumping gas, waiting tables, slaves with white collars. Advertising has us chasing cars and clothes, working jobs we hate so we can buy stuff we don't need. We're the middle children of history, man. No purpose or place. We have no Great War. No Great Depression. Our Great War's a spiritual war ... our Great Depression is our lives.

—Tyler Durden in *Fight Club*

GROUP MEETING

Welcome

Welcome to the first session of *Fight*. If your group members do not yet know one another, introduce yourselves before watching the video.

Video

Play the video segment for Session 1. Use the outline below to help you follow along with the main points, filling in the blanks as you go. (See the appendix for any words you miss.) Jot down any insights or questions for discussion.

NOTES

Men, God created you with a heart of a _____. There are times we must put up a fight, a spiritual fight, where we stand our ground.

Jesus was full of love, grace, mercy ... and he was the greatest warrior who ever lived. In Exodus 15:3, God himself is called a _____.

In Matthew 10:34, Jesus acknowledged he "did not come to bring peace, but a _____."

"I looked for a man among them who would _____ up the wall and _____ before me in the gap on behalf of the land so I would not have to destroy it, but I found none." (Ezekiel 22:30)

Two Principles for Being a Warrior:

1. Every warrior has a _____ to fight for.

   "Don't be _____ of them. Remember the Lord, who is great and awesome, and fight for your families, your sons and your daughters, your wives and your homes." (Nehemiah 4:14)

2. A warrior without a cause to fight _____ will find the wrong thing to fight _____.

   He might fight against authority ... wife ... boss ... boredom. Saul of Tarsus, before he became a Christian, fought against Christianity (see Acts 8:3).

   A warrior without a cause becomes a _____ man.

   When you see a man with godly _____, you will see a man reflecting the _____ of God the Warrior, who stands up for truth.

Two Ways You May Have to Fight:

1. Sometimes, you throw a _____ (metaphorically and spiritually — be active).

   There are times when you have to draw your _____, and your sword is the _____ of God.

   Stand against injustice, stand up for the weak, fight in prayer, leave a job that's hurting you spiritually, or walk away from a woman who is not your wife.

2. Sometimes you turn a _____ (which often takes more strength).

Fight with humility, repentance, _____ your sin, apologizing, asking for _____.

Conclusion: Deuteronomy 20:3–4 says that "the LORD your God is the one who goes _____ you to fight for you against your enemies." The Lord gives you _____. Your job is to _____ ... and fight like a man of God.

Discussion

Take time to discuss what you just watched.

1. In your family of origin, how was "manhood" described and modeled?

2. When you were growing up, what influenced you toward or away from the idea that men are naturally supposed to have a "heart of a warrior"?

How does the challenge of Nehemiah 4:14 line up with or contradict those who influenced you as a boy and shaped your early character?

Describe an early time in your life when you saw your own warrior heart coming out.

3. How do you react to the passage in Exodus 15:3 that describes God as a warrior?

In John 2:13–17, Jesus clears the temple of the moneychangers and animal merchants. He makes a whip, overturns tables, and his language is notably forceful. In what ways do you imagine his anger was like your anger? How might it have been different?

4. Jesus said in Matthew 10:34 that he "didn't come to bring peace but a sword." Yet Jesus is called "the Prince of Peace" in Isaiah

9:6. What kind of "peace" does Jesus not bring, and what kind of peace is he the prince of?

Jesus also said in Matthew 26:52 that "all who draw the sword will die by the sword." What "sword" are we being warned against using, and what exactly is the "sword" Jesus brings in Matthew 10:34?

5. In Ezekiel 22:30, God said, "I looked for someone among them who would build up the wall and stand before me in the gap on behalf of the land so that I would not have to destroy it." What is a "gap"—a place of need and a worthy cause for you to fight for—that brings out your warrior?

Knowing we are susceptible to picking the wrong battles, describe a time when you fought *against* the wrong thing. What price did you pay for that mistake?

6. What is an example from your life of a fight that involved "turning the other cheek"?

What is difficult for you personally when you have to engage in that kind of fight?

Individual Activity: My Takeaway

1. Briefly look over the video outline and any notes you took.

2. In the space below, write down the big idea you want to take away from this meeting. It may be a teaching point you want to sear in your mind or something you sense God wanting you to do.

What I need to focus on as a result of this session is ...

Closing Prayer

Close your meeting with prayer.

PERSONAL STUDY

Reading

Read section 1 of the *Fight* book. Use the space below to note any ideas or questions you want to bring to the next group meeting.

Study

God created men to have the heart of a warrior, placing a desire within us to stand up and fight for what's pure, for what's true. A man has a warrior's heart. You have a warrior's heart. You itch for a fight. That's God's design, not ours.

Fight, page 13

1. People often describe their desired spiritual condition as being filled with "peace" or being completely "at rest" or living in "serenity." While there are certainly biblical precedents for having these worthy aspirations, they don't tell the whole story of our life with God—and they don't capture the essence of what it means to be a man. Many times in Scripture, God wants to stir us up inside, not calm us down. Look up the following passages, and note how you see God actually leading men away

from being at rest and toward a challenge—or fight—of some kind. Put in your own words what you observe:

Genesis 1:28; 2:15

Genesis 12:1–3

Exodus 3:7–12

Luke 22:39–46

John 21:15–19

Acts 9:10–19

Acts 10:9–23

Looking back over these scriptural examples of God-commanded initiative and risk-taking, what might be the role of "peace that passes understanding" (Philippians 4:7) in each situation?

2. What are some aspects of your life or personality that keep you more in status quo mode rather than warrior mode?

What aspect of your own warrior heart do you find hard to accept?

3. What do you think is the difference between having a God-given desire to stand up and fight, and just being a combative person?

Virtually everyone who takes on a fight thinks he is right. Yet we're all human, and too often, we are blind to our own arrogance or self-serving agenda. As Dallas Willard observed, "It is extremely difficult to be right and not hurt anybody with it" (quoted in *God Is Closer Than You Think*, by John Ortberg, page 148). Seeing as that is true, how can we take on a challenging fight without allowing ourselves to be blinded to the possibility we may be in the wrong fight, or fighting in the wrong way?

Who is a good example of a godly fighter that you know or read about, and what makes that person worthy to be emulated?

You're already in a fight, whether you know it or not. Your spiritual enemy wants to take you out. He's a master at making strong men weak. Sometimes he does that by making us comfortable, secure, and safe, resigned to a mediocre life because it's familiar and doesn't require much from us. Is that really how you want to live?

Fight, page 27

4. Read Matthew 13:18−23. As Jesus explains the Parable of the Sower, he mentions three ways in which the seed is rendered unfruitful. Which of those three conditions is most likely to block your spiritual progress? What "fight" would counteract that?

With what "cares of this world" or "deceitfulness of riches" (Matthew 13:22) do you struggle? What steps can you take to overcome their stifling influence?

5. Any of us can fall prey to living according to the values of the world around us. The tragedy is not just the loss of what God could have done through us; it's also that our lives end up being bland and purposeless.

> If you watched a movie about a guy who wanted a Volvo and worked for years to get it, you wouldn't cry at the end when he drove off the lot, testing the windshield wipers. You wouldn't tell your friends you saw a beautiful movie or go home and put a record on to think about the story you'd seen. The truth is, you wouldn't remember that movie a week later, except you'd feel robbed and want your money back. Nobody cries at the

end of a movie about a guy who wants a Volvo. But we spend years actually living those stories, and expect our lives to be meaningful. The truth is, if what we choose to do with our lives won't make a story meaningful, it won't make a life meaningful either.

—Donald Miller, *A Million Miles in a Thousand Years*

What about your life makes "the story of you" meaningful?

What fight are you avoiding that—if you really and truly engaged in it—would turn your life into a story worth telling for generations to come?

Guided Prayer

God, thank you for giving me the heart of a warrior. Show me how I can remove the barriers that keep it from being strong, courageous, and fully yours. Help me get past my fears and insecurities, especially ...

I confess there are times I fight the wrong battles. I can be stubborn, and smug, and sure I'm right. But people I love have told me they see this in me, and when I'm honest, I know they are right and I need to change. Especially help me ...

I also know I sometimes get tired of keeping up with the battles I'm supposed to win. Honestly, I wish some of my problems would just go away—I'm sick of working so hard and not seeing results. But with your help and power, I know I can fight and win, even if it takes the rest of my life. Keep me in the battle, Lord; don't let me give up in these areas ...

I am your warrior, Jesus. I will fight the good fight like a man of God, using the tools of a man of God. When you need a ready man, a good man, or a brave man ... I am here to answer the call. Amen.

///////////////////////////★///////////////////////////

STRONG MEN
WITH WEAK WILLS

///////////////////////////★///////////////////////////

The world has yet to see what God can do through one
man who is wholly surrendered unto him.
> —Spoken by Henry Varley to D. L. Moody

GROUP MEETING

Welcome

Welcome to Session 2 of *Fight*. A key part of growing as a man is sharing life with other men. Before watching the video, briefly check in with each other about what's been going on since the last session. For example:

- How are you doing ... *really?*

- What have you noticed happening in your life or relationship with God that relates to what was discussed in the last session?

- What did you get out of the personal study or your reading in the *Fight* book?

- What questions have come up for you since the last meeting?

Video

Play the video for Session 2. Use the outline below to help you follow along with the main points, filling in the blanks as you go. (See the appendix for any words you miss.) Jot down any insights or questions for discussion.

NOTES

Samson was an incredible warrior who ended up _____ some of the battles that mattered most.

Samson was an incredibly strong man with a dangerously weak _____.

As a boy, he was set apart by God to deliver his people. He took a Nazarite vow (Numbers 6):

- _____ no wine
- Don't eat (touch) any _____ food
- Don't cut _____

But Samson did not live up to his calling—like so many men today. Three attitudes made Samson—and any man—weak:

1. Lust: I _____ it.

   In Judges 14:1−2, he went after a Philistine woman he was forbidden to marry.

2. Entitlement: I _____ it.

   In verses 8−9, he "_____ aside" literally and figuratively to eat honey from a dead lion's carcass.

3. Pride: I can _____ it.

   In verse 10, he held a feast (Hebrew *mishteh*) before his wedding, which literally means a celebration or occasion for drinking.

Samson fell to all three. His selfish and sinful behavior actually caused him to self-destruct.

His actions directly violated two of his Nazarite vows. But in all this, he kept his long hair. He is still making a statement, "Hey, I'm with God," when in reality he's not.

Many people today do the same—metaphorically they still have long hair, but they've lost their intimacy and fellowship with God.

Our spiritual enemy, Satan, loves to make strong men weak. The good news: our God loves to make weak men _____.

Three attitudes that make weak men strong in the Lord:

1. Instead of an "I want it" attitude, we say, "I want _____."

2. Instead of "I deserve it," we realize "I deserve _____" because of sin.

3. Instead of "I can handle it," we say "I can't handle anything _____ God—and with him, I can handle anything."

You don't have to try to be strong in your own power. You can be honest and say, "Without God I'm in big trouble. I don't deserve anything. I need grace. I need his strength."

Conclusion: The good news is, you have the _____ of a warrior; and with the power of Christ, weak though you may be, he will make you strong.

Discussion

Take time to discuss what you just watched.

1. Without naming names, who is a modern-day "Samson" you know (or know of)—a strong man, a spiritually dedicated man, a warrior—but a man who lost his most important battles? What factors led to that man's downfall?

2. What do you believe are your strongest spiritual character qualities—the things that help you be the man you really want to be?

What helps you build and maintain that strength of character? What erodes it?

3. The first attitude that weakens strong men is lust—"I want it." This issue is so universal among men, a popular book addressing it is entitled *Every Man's Battle*. Why do you think lust is so common among men?

Notice that in Judges 14:1–2, Samson initially only took a walk to a nearby town, which is where he saw the woman he wanted. Technically, just visiting the town of Timnah wasn't "wrong," but that's where the temptation overtook him. Similarly, we can engage in activities that might not be technically wrong, but they put us near the sin that is. For you, what is your "Timnah"—the places you go or the things you do that you're able to justify but take you into the vicinity of sin?

4. The second attitude that weakens us is entitlement—"I deserve it." This is an easy fault to see in others but often difficult to see (or admit) in ourselves. Being as truthful as you can, what entitlement are you susceptible to?

If your group members know each other well enough, consider this "graduate-level" follow-up question: Would you be willing to give any man in this group permission to point out an entitlement attitude they see in you—and do that right now?

5. The final attitude that weakens men is pride—"I can handle it." For Samson in Judges 14:10, it was a drinking party. What is your "I can handle it" situation?

While Samson was so physically strong he could kill a lion, being morally strong was exactly what he *wasn't* when it came to women, drinking, and anger (among other issues). Like so many of us, what he is best at is related to what he is vulnerable to. Considering how you answered question 2, where might pride show up in the parts of your character that are strongest? Where else might you be liable to fall if you don't stay vigilant?

Individual Activity: My Takeaway

1. Briefly look over the video outline and any notes you took.

2. In the space below, write down the big idea you want to take away from this meeting. It may be a teaching point you want to sear in your mind or something you sense God wanting you to do.

What I need to focus on as a result of this session is ...

Closing Prayer

Close your meeting with prayer.

PERSONAL STUDY

Reading

Read section 2 of the *Fight* book. Use the space below to note any ideas or questions you want to bring to the next group meeting.

Study

What has God blessed you with that you can identify in your life right now? Before we start looking at how our weaknesses cause us to risk so many of the good things in our lives, it's important to remember what those good things are. You have gifts to use for God's glory. You are chosen and set apart. You have battles to fight. And you have the right weapons to fight with.

Fight, page 39

1. Samson was given very clear signs early in life about the special plans God had for him and what he was to do for the nation once he grew up. Read Judges 13 and note what you find there about the circumstances of his birth and calling:

   The condition of Samson's parents before his conception (vv. 2−3)

The angel's instructions to his mother about his upbringing (v. 5)

What the angel said Samson would do for God once he grew up (v. 5)

What Samson's father did in response to his wife's recounting the message from the angel (vv. 8–12)

His parents' overall spiritual sensitivity and devotion (vv. 19–23)

How God began to manifest his presence in Samson's life even while he was a boy (vv. 24–25)

2. It's likely that God sowed some of the seeds of your calling early in your life, as he did for Samson. Though we cannot claim the miraculous circumstances for our birth comparable

to Samson's, nonetheless God often gives pointers about what he intends for us through our family of origin. He also often manifests abilities and interests in our youth that mature later in life, and which he uses to do his work through us as adults. Take some time to reflect on the following questions, and jot down what comes to mind.

What do I know about each of my parents' families even before they met that is an undeniable part of my heritage? (Note that both good and bad in our family history can be a factor in how God uses us — carrying on a worthy legacy, if good; and breaking a harmful generational pattern, if bad.)

What are the best qualities of my parents — personality traits, skills, character, values, etc. — that have shaped my life even to this day?

What did those who knew me well (parents, relatives, teachers) affirm in me in my younger years?

What did I really enjoy doing as a child, and still enjoy in one form or another to this day?

Which activities or accomplishments really mattered to me— and what was I proud of—when I was a boy?

What was my early sense of "what I wanted to be when I grew up"?

3. As you review your answers to the above questions, in what ways does your life now align with God's early shaping of you?

What step(s) might you take to further live according to his early implanted design for your life?

Men don't plan to destroy themselves. The problem is that we have an enemy who does. His mission statement is to "steal, kill, and destroy" everything that matters to God. Warriors, if you don't have a battle plan, you're going to fall victim to your enemy's battle plan.

Fight, pages 45–46

4. The *Fight* video and book point out three key areas that were at the core of Samson's downfall: lust, entitlement, and pride. They trouble most men today as well. In fact, without a battle plan, they will do more than trouble you—they will take you out. In light of that sobering reality, let's put together a simple battle plan in each of these areas:

LUST ("I want it")
Circumstances in which I am most vulnerable:

Note: As you consider your own vulnerabilities, it may help to use the acronym "H.A.L.T.", which stands for "hungry, angry, lonely, tired"; addiction counselors point out that those conditions most easily lead to acting out.

Ways I rationalize allowing myself to go near—or even into—settings where I can fall (i.e., common things I do that aren't the sin, but lead to it):

The price I would pay—or have paid—for giving in to lust:

Bible passages (and themes) I can read, remind myself of, or memorize that strengthen my commitment to purity:

For example, check out Job 31:1; Proverbs 5:3–23; 6:20–7:27; Matthew 5:27–30; 1 Corinthians 6:13–20; 10:12–13; Galatians 6:8–9; Ephesians 5:3–14; 1 Thessalonians 4:3–8; 2 Timothy 2:22; Titus 2:11–12; Hebrews 4:15–16; 1 Peter 1:13–16.

Men I can call any time, day or night, when I need support:

ENTITLEMENT ("I deserve it")

Entitlement attitudes I see in others, which tick me off:

Ways those things I just wrote down are actually true of me sometimes:

Rules, laws, or procedures that I think I shouldn't have to follow and that I sometimes disregard or "bend" for my benefit:

For example: Obeying speed limits, punctuality, tax requirements, having to keep all of my agreements, what I do (or don't do) if people are watching but do the opposite if they aren't, things I keep from my wife or close friends because "they wouldn't understand," etc.

Regrets I now have over actions I took because I thought to myself, "I deserve it":

Ways I would be a better man if I gave up my presumed entitlement prerogatives:

PRIDE ("I can handle it")

Ask 100 people to rate themselves in any category (a specific skill, attractiveness, maturity, intelligence, productivity, etc.) with the scale "better than average, average, or below average" and the results are always the same: more people rate themselves "better than average" than is possible (you can't have 75 percent of people "better than average" by definition!). This is called the "self-serving bias"—the way in which we falsely attribute positive outcomes to our own actions or abilities and resist owning the extent to which we contribute to our failures. Another word for this is *pride*, and the Bible warns us of its pitfalls.

Situations in which my pride overrode good judgment:

Prideful attitudes in me that others have pointed out:

Some lessons about pride from Scripture:

Proverbs 8:13

Proverbs 11:2

Proverbs 16:18

Proverbs 29:23

Isaiah 13:11

1 John 2:16

Without God, I ... *(complete this sentence several times with different personal examples to remind you of what happens when you push God aside and let pride rule your life)*:

Guided Prayer

God, thank you for putting so many good things into my life: good influences, good gifts, good training. Specifically, I thank you for ...

I acknowledge my many weaknesses. Like Samson, I've sometimes allowed lust, entitlement, and pride to get the best of me. I want to confess right now ...

Thank you for giving me a battle plan to stay connected to you. Strengthen me to follow the lessons I've learned in this study. Remind me of the cost of failing, and the blessings that are mine when I win these battles. With your help, I will turn "I want it" to "I want you"; "I deserve it" to "I deserve death"; and "I can handle it" to "I can't handle anything without you." Amen.

SPIRIT-LED, NOT EMO-DRIVEN

Sometimes I think there's a beast that lives inside me, in the cavern that's where my heart should be, and every now and then it fills every last inch of my skin, so that I can't help but do something inappropriate. Its breath is full of lies; it smells of spite.

—Jodi Picoult, *Handle with Care*

GROUP MEETING

Welcome

Welcome to Session 3 of *Fight*. A key part of growing as a man is sharing life with other men. Before watching the video, briefly check in with each other about what's been going on since the last session. For example:

- How are you doing ... *really?*

- What have you noticed happening in your life or relationship with God that relates to what was discussed in the last session?

- What did you get out of the personal study or your reading in the *Fight* book?

- What questions have come up for you since the last meeting?

Video

Play the video for Session 3. Use the outline below to help you follow along with the main points, filling in the blanks as you go. (See the appendix for any words you miss.) Jot down any insights or questions for discussion.

NOTES

Samson had a supernatural _____ from God and was set apart with supernatural strength, but he had a dangerously weak will.

Samson was _____-driven, not Spirit-led.

Both men and women are emotional, but show it in _____

ways. When women are emotional, they _____; men tend to
_____.

This gets us in trouble when we know what's right, but we do
what we feel like doing rather than what's right.

Galatians 5:16 – 17, "So I say to live by the Spirit and you will
not gratify the desires of the sinful nature. For the sinful nature
desires what's _____ to the Spirit and the Spirit what is
contrary to the sinful nature. They're in _____ with each
other so you do not do what you want."

Samson made a stupid bet with thirty Philistines (who were
the enemy), giving them a riddle (Judges 14:14). When they
couldn't figure it out, they pressed his bride-to-be to trick him
into revealing the answer.

Emotions we need to learn to fight and defeat:
1. **Fight your burning _____.**
   It's not a _____ to be angry, it's a sin to act on your anger
   in the _____ way. After losing the bet, Samson set off an
   anger-filled, violent chain reaction:

   • Samson used the strength God gave him to kill thirty
     innocent men to make good on his promise.

   • While on his killing spree, Samson's wife-to-be was given to
     the friend, who had attended him, to marry in his absence.

   • Samson was furious, so he tied some foxes' tails together
     with torches to run through and destroy the Philistines'
     harvest.

   • The Philistines retaliated for the destruction of their
     harvest; they killed the girl and burned her father to death.

Samson's anger not only cost him, but it cost those that he
_____. Our anger can do the same.

For many of us, anger is a default emotion. Embarrassment or pain produces an angry reaction.

What did Samson have to be angry about? He's the guy who made all the choices; in reality, it's almost all his own fault.

Men with great potential let the emotion of anger go wild. Sometimes their anger is directed at themselves as they take it out on the rest of the world. Anger gone wild can take a strong man down.

2. **Fight your personal _____.**
Samson killed a thousand men, using the strength of God, and then boasted about it.

Pride is born out of our _____. The more insecure we are, the more we try to _____ with pride.

If you let your _____ drive you to God, God will _____ your deepest need. Samson took his physical thirst to God, and also acknowledged that God was behind his strength, and he was revived.

Conclusion: God has given you the heart of a warrior, and you've lost some battles and done some stupid things. If you will _____ yourself and say, "I need God, I need your grace," he will give you strength and you will be _____. Our good God loves to make weak men strong.

Discussion

Take time to discuss what you just watched.

1. As Craig noted in the video, there tend to be differences in how the sexes process emotions — women verbally and men

through actions. How did that hold true among the adult men and women in your family growing up?

It's also true that sometimes men are verbal and women more demonstrative. Where do *you* fit along that continuum in how you typically show strong emotions?

2. What is an example of your anger in action recently? What factors tend to make you so mad you do things you regret?

3. Ephesians 4:26 says, "Be angry and do not sin; do not let the sun go down on your anger." What does non-sinful anger look like?

What does it mean practically to "not let the sun go down on your anger"? What makes that practice hard for you personally?

4. In Romans 8:6 – 8, a passage similar in theme to Galatians 5:16 – 17 that Craig discusses in the video, the apostle Paul writes: "The mind governed by the flesh is death, but the mind governed by the Spirit is life and peace. The mind governed by the flesh is hostile to God; it does not submit to God's law, nor can it do so. Those who are in the realm of the flesh cannot please God." What is your reaction to Paul's point that our minds, if governed by "the flesh," have *no ability whatsoever* to do what God wants?

If that is so, how do we both use our minds and emotions, which are gifts from God, and yet also live by the power of the Spirit of God?

5. The root of pride is not too much belief in our goodness, but rather insecurity and a need to compensate for our lack of confidence and wounded self-esteem. As Søren Kierkegaard pointed out, "The proud person always wants to do the right thing, the great thing. But because he wants to do it in his own strength, he is fighting not with man, but with God."

Looking back on an episode of pride, in what way can you now admit that you were "fighting with God" — and doing so because of insecurity?

6. Craig said, "If you let your need drive you to God, God will meet your deepest need." What need in you has driven you to God recently?

In what ways have you felt God meeting that need?

In what ways does that need still feel unmet?

Individual Activity: My Takeaway

1. Briefly look over the outline and any notes you took.

2. In the space below, write down the big idea you want to take away from this meeting and what it motivates you to do.

What I've learned from this session— and where I need to fight the good fight like a man— is . . .

Closing Prayer

Close your meeting with prayer.

PERSONAL STUDY

Reading

Read section 3 of the *Fight* book. Use the space below to note any ideas or questions you want to bring to the next group meeting.

Study

> For most men, talking doesn't feel like it accomplishes anything. "Doing" does. The problem is that when we let our emotions lead us to do something, often it is something we shouldn't have done.
>
> ★ *Fight*, page 67

1. Jesus was no stranger to emotions. Read the following verses and note the emotions you see him experiencing:

   John 11:35; Luke 19:41; Isaiah 53:3

   Mark 3:4 – 5; 10:14; John 2:13 – 17

Mark 15:33–34; Luke 22:42–44

Luke 10:21; John 3:29

Matthew 9:36; Mark 1:40–41; John 11:33, 38

2. One way to categorize core emotions is to use the acronym S.A.S.H.E.T., which stands for "Sad, Angry, Scared, Happy, Excited, Tender." Other emotions are variations of these base-level feelings (with more or less intensity). None are "bad"; our feelings just exist and are morally neutral. How we react to our feelings is what gets us into trouble, because our emotions are good servants, but bad rulers. As you think about your own life experience, use the following chart to reflect on the role emotions have played, both good and bad (and don't worry if you don't have an example for every box).

Emotion/ Related Terms	How It Has Helped Me	Ways I've Misused It
Sad (grief, sorrow, unhappy, bereaved, downcast, melancholy, sense of loss)		
Angry (mad, annoyed, displeased, infuriated, violated, blocked)		

continued

Emotion/ Related Terms	How It Has Helped Me	Ways I've Misused It
Scared (fear, terror, anxious, alarm, apprehensive, worry, dread, concern, threatened)		
Happy (joy, elation, cheerful, delighted, peaceful, upbeat, glad, blessed, laugh)		
Excited (animated, eager, anticipation, fired up, looking forward, pumped, thrilled)		
Tender (moved, connected, soft, feeling love, vulnerable, touched, caring, sentimental)		

3. Of all the feelings, anger seems to be one most likely to get us men into trouble from time to time. Consider these observations about anger:

> "How much more grievous are the consequences of anger than the causes of it."
>
> —Marcus Aurelius, *Meditations*

> "Never respond to an angry person with a fiery comeback, even if he deserves it … Don't allow his anger to become your anger."
>
> —Bohdi Sanders, *Warrior Wisdom: Ageless Wisdom for the Modern Warrior*

How would you put the above ideas into your own words?

Growing up, how did your male role models confirm the truth of these statements—either positively or negatively?

Pride is always born of our insecurities. When we don't know who we are in Christ, we use pride to try to fill that void.
Fight, page 80

★

4. A key verse about pride is Proverbs 21:24. Here is the text in several translations:

The proud and arrogant man—"Mocker" is his name; he behaves with overweening pride. (New International Version)

Mockers are proud and haughty; they act with boundless arrogance. (New Living Translation)

"Scoffer" is the name of the arrogant, haughty man who acts with arrogant pride. (English Standard Version)

Although harsh words are used to describe a prideful person in these translations, most of us can relate to times when we've acted with pride. Describe a time when pride turned you into a "mocker" or "scoffer."

5. C. S. Lewis wrote in *Mere Christianity*:

> A proud man is always looking down on things and people; and, of course, as long as you are looking down, you cannot see something that is above you ... Pride gets no pleasure out of having something, only out of having more of it than the next man ... It is the comparison that makes you proud: the pleasure of being above the rest. Once the element of competition is gone, pride is gone.

Who or what do you tend to compare yourself to (look down on) that fuels and reveals your pride?

How is "knowing who you are in Christ" an antidote to that pride?

6. Craig noted that despair can also be a form of pride. He writes:

> We get stuck in these negative loops of self-judgment and con-
> demnation that are not from God. His Spirit always leads us to
> confession, to changing directions and going God's way, to a
> fresh start, to grace. Often God has forgiven us, but our emo-
> tions haven't caught up. I'm convinced this is just another form
> of our pride — wanting to be in control of ourselves and not
> rely on God. We'd rather hate ourselves than risk the vulnera-
> bility and humility required to depend on him. It seems easier
> to expect the worst than to put our hope in God. (*Fight*, pages
> 83–84)

Describe a situation when you felt pride keeping you from fully embracing God's forgiveness. What price did you pay for not allowing his love in?

Guided Prayer

God, thank you for giving me emotions. Thank you too for giving me a model in Jesus of how to feel and express the full range of human emotions. Open me up to the feelings I tend to avoid, especially . . .

I confess that, like Samson, my anger and pride bring harm to others and myself. Forgive me, Lord, for the following angry or prideful actions and the hurt I caused . . .

I commit again to allowing your Spirit to lead me, and not letting my feelings control me. Thank you for living in me so I have the power I need. I will humbly ask for help when I need it—from you and from others—so that I do not allow anger, pride, or despair to rule and ruin my life. Amen.

///////////////////////////////★///////////////////////////////

SMALL STEPS, BIG DESTRUCTION

///////////////////////////////★///////////////////////////////

No man ever became extremely wicked all at once.
—Juvenal, *Satires II* (Roman poet, circa AD 140)

GROUP MEETING

Welcome

Welcome to Session 4 of *Fight*. A key part of growing as a man is sharing life with other men. Before watching the video, briefly check in with each other about what's been going on since the last session. For example:

- How are you doing ... *really*?

- What have you noticed happening in your life or relationship with God that relates to what was discussed in the last session?

- What did you get out of the personal study or your reading in the *Fight* book?

- What questions have come up for you since the last meeting?

Video

Play the video for Session 4. Use the outline below to help you follow along with the main points, filling in the blanks as you go. (See the appendix for any words you miss.) Jot down any insights or questions for discussion.

NOTES

After his previous mistakes, for the next twenty years Samson led Israel as an effective leader. But even though it looked like he was on the right track, apparently he just buried his problems, ignored them, or did what so many of us do — cover up his deeper issues and not deal with them.

Most men don't ruin their lives all at _____; they do it one _____ at a time.

One day Samson went to see a prostitute. It was about twenty-five miles away in Gaza, so he took 56,250 steps in the direction of danger—and he had 56,250 _____ to stop and say "This is not worth it," and turn around and go back.

There are three steps that often we fall victim to and lose the battle:

1. **We think we can handle it, so we _____ our enemy.**

   • Satan is our enemy, a roaring lion seeking someone to _____.

   • Christianity is not a playground; it's a _____.

   • We put ourselves in stupid places. We flirt with danger.

2. **We _____ the same sin over and over.**

   • Samson is vulnerable to women, and now he seeks out a Philistine woman: Delilah.

   • The Philistines want her to find out the secret to Samson's strength. The text says, "With such nagging she prodded him day after day until he was tired to death." She wears him down and finally learns the secret is his long hair.

   • Samson, like us, is strong in many other areas, but he's not strong enough to _____ a woman.

   • Too often, we're not strong enough to lay down our lives to serve and love, and honor, and nurture, and lead to where we're all _____ to God.

3. **We _____ disobedience won't cost us.**

   • Samson assumed he would get away with it again. But they caught him, gouged out his eyes, and put him to work grinding in the prison.

Warriors, there's a fight you may need to win. There is a battle that matters. Where have you stepped away from God?

You are only as strong as you are _____.

If you've stepped away from him ... if you're going the wrong way, what do you do? You _____ around. God will be right there to welcome you.

Conclusion: Samson's strength was in his hair, and it began to grow again after it had been shaved. That symbolizes _____. God says, "If you turn back to me, I will forgive every sin that you've ever committed, and I will make you new. I specialize in _____ stories." The enemy loves to make strong men weak, but God loves to make weak men strong.

Discussion

Take time to discuss what you just watched.

1. Early in the video, Craig said, "Men don't ruin their lives all at once; they do it one step at a time." A vivid illustration of this is found in Proverbs 7:6–27. Read those verses, and notice in verse 22 that it says the young man followed "all at once." Yet how many steps can you identify that the young man took *before* his final step of falling?

Describe a moral or personal "crash"—either from your life experience or someone you know—that illustrates the truth of many steps preceding a fall. (It's not necessary to share names.)

What is it about our human nature that causes us *not* to guard against the small steps that lead toward ruin? Why do we even need this reminder, when it seems so obvious?

2. After twenty years of good leadership and integrity, why do you think a man like Samson would just head over to Gaza (enemy territory—and the "red light district" of his day) and sleep with a prostitute?

Read 1 Corinthians 10:12. In Samson's case, twenty years of good behavior didn't solidify his character enough to prevent a moral fall. What do you think will keep you from a similar fate?

3. The first dangerous step Samson took was to taunt his enemy—to enter enemy territory and act as if he were invulnerable. In what ways do you find yourself engaging in risky, spiritual-enemy-taunting behavior?

What chancy situations have you been drawn to recently, and why?

4. The second dangerous step Samson took was to rationalize his sin. What rationalizations of sin are you prone to make?

What is the hard reality that you don't want to admit—the reality which your rationalizations are an attempt to mask?

5. The final lesson from this part of Samson's life is how he told himself he'd get away with it — that his disobedience wouldn't cost him. What price have you paid for disobedience that you thought you wouldn't have to?

6. In the video, Craig said: "You are only as strong as you are honest." Describe a time when you or someone you know demonstrated strength through radical honesty.

Individual Activity: My Takeaway

1. Briefly look over the outline and any notes you took.

2. In the space below, write down the big idea you want to take away from this meeting and what it motivates you to do.

What I've learned from this session — and where I need to fight the good fight like a man — is ...

Closing Prayer

Close your meeting with prayer.

PERSONAL STUDY

Reading

Read section 4 of the *Fight* book. Use the space below to note any ideas or questions you want to bring to the next group meeting.

Study

> Your enemy hates your guts. Do you get that? He despises you. Why? Because he hates everything that matters to God, and nothing matters more to God than you. Your enemy is a worthy adversary. His name is Satan. The Bible calls him the father of lies. He's the great deceiver. And he wants to destroy you.
>
> *Fight,* page 117

★

1. Although we are often our own worst enemy, we have another spiritual enemy—Satan—who uses our weaknesses against us. What do the following passages teach about him and his schemes? Draw a circle around the reference that you most want to keep in mind in the coming days.

John 8:44

Acts 5:3

Romans 16:19−20

1 Corinthians 7:5

2 Corinthians 11:14

Ephesians 4:26−27

James 4:7

1 Peter 5:6−10

1 John 5:19

Revelation 12:9−11

2. What do you think are the similarities as well as differences between fighting battles against your own sinful tendencies and fighting battles against Satan?

> Like Samson, we don't mess up our lives all at once. We do it one step at a time. We doom ourselves when we taunt the enemy, when we rationalize our sin, and then when we assume that our disobedience isn't going to cost us anything. We forget that our sin always takes us farther than we want to go and costs us more than we want to pay.
>
> *Fight*, page 111

3. Samson's three steps toward failure were taunting the enemy, rationalizing sin, and assuming disobedience wouldn't cost him. Use the following chart to consider your own propensities, the cost of those, and what you want to do instead:

Step Toward Failure	How I Do That	Eventual Results	New Behavior I Choose
Taunt the Enemy			
Rationalize Sin			
Assume Disobedience Won't Cost Me			

4. All of us are prone to step away from God from time to time. In the words of the hymn "Come, Thou Fount of Every Blessing":

Let thy goodness, like a fetter,
Bind my wandering heart to thee.
Prone to wander, Lord, I feel it,
Prone to leave the God I love;
Here's my heart, O take and seal it,
Seal it for thy courts above.

The book *Fight* noted several ways we commonly step away from God (pages 113–114), which are listed below. Where are you on the continuum for each one right now?

	Not an Issue	Rarely a Problem	Sometimes a Problem	Often a Problem	I'm in Big Trouble
Not spending time in God's Word	1	2	3	4	5
Not spending time in prayer	1	2	3	4	5
Lust	1	2	3	4	5
Anger	1	2	3	4	5
Apathy and passive living	1	2	3	4	5
Greed	1	2	3	4	5

Which one do you want to focus on changing in the coming days?

What's a step you'll take *this week* to move back toward God in this area?

5. Craig noted in the *Fight* book that sometimes we feel emasculated and stifle the spirit of the warrior that God placed within us. When we feel stripped of power, it's easier to give in to temptation. What is a way you need to step into your power — God's warrior power within you — to fight for something or someone in need of your holy strength?

Take heart from these encouraging words:

What battle are you facing? Give it a name.

Marriage crumbling? Draw your sword. Fight. Don't surrender. It's a cause that's beyond yourself.

Kids turning away from God? Pray them back to God. Use God's weapons.

Drowning financially? Fight. Discipline yourself to start winning small battles.

Surrounded on every side by your sin? Unleash the warrior's heart inside of you. Fight. Romans 8:37 says we are "more than conquerors through [Christ] who loved us." We overcome, Revelation tells us, by the blood of the Lamb and by the words of our testimonies. Our strength is not our own. We can do all things through Christ who strengthens us.

You have the heart of a warrior. Nothing can distract you. People cannot disillusion you. Critics cannot derail you. Demons cannot stop you.

You are a man. God gave you a cause to inspire you. Honor it. God gave you weapons to fight for it. Face your fear. Tell the truth. Fight, and fight to win. You're ready, you have permission, and you're not alone. It's time to quit walking blindly through your life falling into the traps of your enemy.

It's time to turn around and fight for your life.

Fight, page 121

Guided Prayer

God, thank you for encouraging me to stay in the fight. Thank you for giving me power over Satan. Specifically, I pray you would deal him a decisive blow and give me victory in these areas ...

I know I need to turn to you. I commit again to applying Spirit-empowered effort toward those areas in my life where I am drifting away. I confess openly and honestly that I ...

Thank you for making me a man and for giving me a warrior's heart. I commit again, under your leadership and in the power of the Holy Spirit, to live and lead from the core of who I am. I want people in my world to be drawn to you, and to take back a little more territory each day—ground that has been lost to the evil one. As I fight, let me bring all of myself—along with any others to whom you lead me—back into the loving presence and power of your kingdom. In Jesus' name, Amen.

////////////////////////////////////★////////////////////////////////////

FAILING FORWARD

////////////////////////////////////★////////////////////////////////////

No human ever became interesting by not failing. The more you fail and recover and improve, the better you are as a person. Ever meet someone who's ALWAYS had EVERYTHING work out for them with ZERO struggle? They usually have the depth of a puddle. Or they don't exist.

—Chris Hardwick, *The Nerdist Way: How to Reach the Next Level (In Real Life)*

GROUP MEETING

Welcome

Welcome to Session 5 of *Fight*. A key part of growing as a man is sharing life with other men. Before watching the video, briefly check in with each other about what's been going on since the last session. For example:

- How are you doing ... *really?*

- What have you noticed happening in your life or relationship with God that relates to what was discussed in the last session?

- What did you get out of the personal study or your reading in the *Fight* book?

- What questions have come up for you since the last meeting?

Video

Play the video for Session 5. Use the outline below to help you follow along with the main points, filling in the blanks as you go. (See the appendix for any words you miss.) Jot down any insights or questions for discussion.

NOTES

What do you do when you've blown it? We men tend to get our value from what we accomplish, what we do.

A man's greatest fear is _____ and greatest pain is _____. If we can't win, we don't want to play.

A failure is an _____, never a _____.

Samson is blind, captive, and a laughingstock. The Philistines are sacrificing to their god, Dagon, and praising him for delivering Samson into their hands.

Two responses to failure: the natural response is _____, the godly response is _____.

Remorse is "I feel _____." We try to shift _____.

Repentance is "I was _____." It is honest enough to say, "I'm _____." But we can't undo what we did.

Remorse is looking _____. Repentance is turning to _____. You are not what you _____. You are who God says you are.

Samson steps across a line of commitment: "Never again is it about me." The calling of God doesn't go away. Turn around and come back to God.

Samson asks for strength "just once more." We may be _____, but we're not _____.

Even in our _____, God can still accomplish his purposes.

What _____ do you need to push down? Pride? Entitlement? Financial irresponsibility? Lust? Passive relationship with wife? Not there for kids?

How are you going to do it? Name the pillar that's going down, and seek God.

God has called you to greatness. You have the _____ of a warrior. Don't just fight like a man; fight like a man of God.

Samson gave his life _____ time. A man of God gives his life _____.

Conclusion: You can be a great hero and a great man of God when it's not about you. Satan loves to make strong men weak, but you're a warrior; there's fight in you; there are some battles that you must win and win decisively. The Spirit of God within you will help you win; the world has yet to see what God can do through one man wholly surrendered to him. You can be that man. You can fight, not just like a man, but you can fight like a man of God. By the power of Christ, you will be victorious.

Discussion

Take time to discuss what you just watched.

1. Describe a recent screwup. To what extent did you feel that your value as a man — your accomplishments, what you achieve, needing to win — was affected by that?

2. Craig said in the video: "Our greatest fear is failure and greatest pain is regret." What is your reaction to that statement? If you have a different greatest fear or greatest pain, what is it for you?

3. Of the two responses to failure—remorse or repentance—which are you more likely to do? Why do you think you go more toward that one?

4. Proverbs 24:16 says, "Though the righteous fall seven times, they rise again, but the wicked stumble when calamity strikes." If someone is righteous, why does he fall so much? And how is that any different from what happens to the wicked?

5. Craig said, "You are not what you did; you are who God says you are." When do you find yourself tempted to put too much value on what you did (positive or negative)?

Of all the things that God says you are, which are most important to you as a corrective to that wrong self-assessment?

6. Read Luke 9:23 and 1 Corinthians 15:31. For you, what does "taking up your cross" and "dying daily" mean, practically speaking? How does someone "fight like a man — as a hero" and at the same time "die daily"?

7. As this study draws to a close, reflect on what you've experienced together as a group by doing the following:

   • One man volunteers to go first.

   • Start by speaking to the man on your left, and finish this sentence with a phrase: "What I most respect about you being in this group is …"

   • Go around the group, completing the sentence for each man.

   • Finish by briefly explaining how God is stretching you (or by describing a battle that you were losing but are now winning).

   • Do this until every man has had an opportunity to express his one-phrase of admiration for every man present.

Individual Activity: My Takeaway

1. Briefly look over the outline and any notes you took.

2. In the space below, write down the big idea you want to take away from this meeting and what it motivates you to do.

   What I've learned from this session— and where I need to fight the good fight like a man— is …

CLOSING PRAYER

Close your meeting with prayer.

PERSONAL STUDY

Reading

Read section 5 of the *Fight* book. Use the space below to note any ideas or questions.

Study

> God didn't make us to be warriors so that we'd be perfect; he made us to be warriors so that we'd fight our fears, learn from our mistakes, and live to fight another day.
>
> *Fight*, page 127

1. What fear is keeping you from being the warrior God made you to be?

What's a recent mistake that you made, and what are you learning from it?

Assuming you could get past your fear(s) and mistake(s), what "fight" would you enter that you're holding back from?

2. When the Israelites first wanted to enter the land to conquer it, they sent out twelve spies to see what they were up against. Two of the spies were sure that with God's help, they would prevail. But the rest of the spies had a different take. Read Numbers 13:31 – 33 for what the other ten said.

Notice in the story the effect of fear on their perception of reality: in their terror, the spies exaggerated the problem, and thought of themselves as mere "grasshoppers." But according to verse 33, who first saw the spies as grasshoppers — the Nephilim, or the spies themselves? What might that indicate about the way our view of ourselves can also affect the way others see us?

Think about your marriage, your coworkers, your profession, or even the men in your small group. In what way are you seeing yourself as a "grasshopper" — a small or less-than person? How do you think that is affecting the way others see you?

> If you think God uses only perfect people,
> then you haven't read the Bible. Or you
> haven't been paying attention to the people
> all around you who are making a difference
> in this world every day. Only once did God
> ever use a perfect person. Before then
> and ever since ... he has worked with
> whatever we have given him.
>
> *Fight*, pages 133–134

★

3. How would you explain to a new Christian that God wants us to be pure and holy so he can use us, but also that he uses us when we are weak and imperfect?

4. What light does 2 Corinthians 12:9–10 shed on this issue?

What weakness in you has God used to show his power?

> Remorse is a common response to failure, but there's a much better one: repentance. Instead of turning inward or deflecting outward, you turn upward. Instead of allowing yourself to get stuck, you stop and then let God move you through it. You drop the guilt, the regret, the anger, and the self-pity and return to the Lord ... Remorse builds an emotional monument to our sin, then stands there gazing at it while we feel bad. Repentance is turning one hundred and eighty degrees away from our sin and then walking away from it.
>
> ★ *Fight*, page 138

5. How would you describe your own tendencies toward remorse instead of repentance?

Is there any remorse you feel stuck in right now? If so, what's a repentance step you could take instead?

6. Repentance requires clarity — knowing exactly what you're turning away from. The metaphor used in the Samson story was about pushing on the "pillars" — those things holding

up what has been ruling, oppressing, and tormenting us. The *Fight* book and video challenged us to name those pillars that need to come down.

Read 1 John 1:9. "Confess" just means to agree with—in this context, agree with God about our sins (the pillars that hold us). What pillars are in your life that you "agree with God" need to be pushed down? On a separate piece of paper, name them one by one. When you've done that, get a Sharpie and write out the words of 1 John 1:9 in bold, block letters over those things that have been named and forgiven. Then destroy that list as a final testimony to what God has done.

Read James 5:16. *Confessing* gets us forgiveness; *confessing to others* helps us heal. To whom do you need to confess a wrong you've done? By when will you do that?

Even if you don't need to confess a particular offense against an individual, confessing to another person can bring into the light what has been hidden, so fresh air can blow through your soul and bring healing. Who could you talk to (preferably other than your spouse) so you can name honestly and specifically your pillars? By when will you contact that person to do that?

Guided Prayer

God, thank you that failure is not final. Thank you that with every mistake I've made or sin I've committed, you are there to take me back. Thank you for showing me that truth in Samson's life. God, right now I want to turn every area of my life back to you, including my failures and mistakes such as ...

At times, I've chosen things other than repentance, including remorse. Help me not to focus so much on myself, but instead to own what I've done and move on. When I'm tempted to get bogged down in just feeling bad, show me the way out. Right now, I feel remorse over the following things, and with your help, I want to release the sorrow and fully repent ...

Thank you for putting the heart of a warrior in me. Show me what battles to fight. Show me how to fight in the power of your Spirit, and not as the world fights. You came through for Samson; come through for me. All of who I am is yours to use for your purposes in the world, so help me fight with your strength, and fight to win. Amen.

VIDEO NOTES ANSWER KEY

SESSION 1:
Fight Like a Man

warrior	sword, Word
warrior	cheek
sword	owning, help
build, stand	with, victory, fight
cause	
afraid	
for, against	
destructive	
important	
strength, goodness	
punch	

SESSION 2:
Strong Men
with Weak Wills

losing

will

drink, unclean, hair

want, deserve, turned,
handle

strong

God, death, without

heart

SESSION 3:
Spirit-Led,
Not Emo-Driven

calling

emotion

different, talk, act

contrary, conflict

anger

sin, wrong

loved

pride

insecurities, compensate

need, meet

humble, revived

SESSION 4:
Small Steps, Big Destruction

once, step

opportunities

taunt, devour,
battleground

rationalize, lead, closer

assume

honest

turn

grace, turnaround

SESSION 5:
Failing Forward

failure, regret

event, person

remorse, repentance

bad, blame

wrong, sorry

backward, God, did

down, out

failures

pillars

heart

one, daily

Fight

Winning the Battles
That Matter Most

Craig Groeschel

Author and pastor Craig Groeschel helps you uncover who you really are — a man created in the image of God with a warrior's heart — and how to fight the good fight for what's right. You will find the strength to fight the battles you know you need to fight — the ones that determine the state of your heart, the quality of your marriage, and the spiritual health of your family.

Craig will also look at examples from the Bible, including our good buddy Samson. Yep, the dude with the rippling biceps, hippie hair, and a thing for Delilah. You may be surprised how much we have in common with this guy. By looking at his life, you'll learn how to defeat the demons that make strong men weak. You'll become who God made you to be:

A man who knows how to fight for what's right.

And don't you dare show up for this fight unarmed. Learn how to fight with faith, with prayer, and with the Word of God

It's time to fight like a man. For God's Sake, FIGHT.

Altar Ego: A DVD Study

Becoming Who God Says You Are

Craig Groeschel

You are *not* who you think you are. In fact, according to bestselling author Craig Groeschel, you need to take your idea of your own identity, lay it down on the altar, and sacrifice it. Give it to God. Offer it up.

Why? Because you are who God says you are. And until you've sacrificed your broken concept of your identity, you won't become who you are meant to be.

When we place our false labels and self-deception on the altar of God's truth, we discover who we really are as his sons and daughters. Instead of an outward-driven, approval-based ego, we learn to live with an "altar ego," God's vision of who we are becoming.

Discover how to trade in your broken ego and unleash your altar ego to become a living sacrifice. Once we know our true identity and are growing in Christlike character, then we can behave accordingly, with bold behavior, bold prayers, bold words, and bold obedience.

Altar Ego reveals who God says you are, and then calls you to live up to it.

Small Group Curriculum Also Available:
- 5-Session DVD – 9780310894933
- Study Guide – 9780310894940
- Study Guide with DVD – 9780310693031

Available in stores and online!

Soul Detox: A DVD Study

Clean Living in a Contaminated World

Craig Groeschel

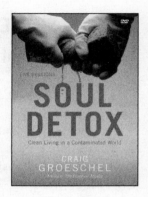

In *Soul Detox*, pastor and bestselling author Craig Groeschel sheds light on relationships, thoughts, and behaviors that quietly compromise our well-being. Through concise teaching and honest humor, Groeschel provides a source of inspiration and encouragement for a faith-filled lifestyle that will keep you free of spiritual toxins.

Our culture unknowingly ingests regular doses of spiritual toxins that assault our relationship with God. This five-session small-group DVD Bible study with participant's guide (sold separately) shines light on dark influences, emotions, and behaviors in order to empower Christians to live pure lives and grow closer to God.

Sessions include:

1. *Lethal Language:* Experiencing the Power of Life-Giving Words
2. *Scare Pollution:* Unlocking the Chokehold of Fear
3. *Radioactive Relationships:* Loving Unhealthy People without Getting Sick
4. *Septic Thoughts:* Overcoming Our False Beliefs
5. *Germ Warfare:* Cleansing Our Lives of Cultural Toxins

Soul Detox can be used in a variety of ways — as a whole church campaign (adult congregation), as an adult Sunday school study, as a small group study, or for individual Bible study. The DVD contains five 10 to 15 minute video teaching sessions from pastor Craig Groeschel, and the participant's guide provides individual and group activities, between-session personal studies, and additional background material that will enhance the experience of the video sessions.

Weird: A DVD Study

Because Normal Isn't Working

Craig Groeschel

In this six-session small group DVD Bible study (participant's guide sold separately), pastor and bestselling author Craig Groeschel shatters "normal" and turns "weird" upside down.

Normal people are stressed, overwhelmed, and exhausted. Many of their relationships are, at best, strained and, in most cases, just surviving. Even though we live in one of the most prosperous places on earth, normal is still living paycheck to paycheck and never getting ahead.

Lust and frequent "casual" sex are far more common than purity and a healthy married sex life. And when it comes to God, many believe, but few practice the teachings of Scripture in their everyday lives.

Simply put, normal isn't working. Craig Groeschel's WEIRD views will help you break free from the norm to lead a radically abnormal (and endlessly more fulfilling) life.

Available in stores and online!

The Christian Atheist: A DVD Study

Believing in God but Living as If He Doesn't Exist

Craig Groeschel

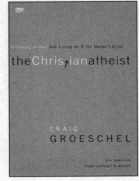

In this six-session small group DVD Bible study (participant's guide sold separately), pastor and bestselling author Craig Groeschel leads you and your group on a personal journey toward an authentic, God-honoring life. This honest, hard-hitting, and eye-opening look into the ways people believe in God but live as if he doesn't exist is a classic in the making.

You believe in God, attend church when it's convenient, and you generally treat people with kindness. But, have you surrendered to God completely, living every day depending upon the Holy Spirit?

Craig Groeschel encourages you and your group to be more than just "Christian" in name, to be honest before God, and to break free of hypocrisy to live a more authentic, God-honoring life.

Available in stores and online!